Pursuit

Pursuit

Erica Funkhouser

A Mariner Book
Houghton Mifflin Company
Boston   New York

First Mariner Books edition 2004

Visit our Web site: www.houghtonmifflinbooks.com.

Library of Congress Cataloging-in-Publication Data
Funkhouser, Erica.
    Pursuit / Erica Funkhouser.
        p.   cm.
    ISBN 0-618-17152-5
    ISBN 0-618-38187-2 (pbk.)
    I. Title.
PS3556.U63 P87   2002
811'.54—dc21   2001051619

Book design by Melissa Lotfy
Typeface: Monotype Ehrhardt

Printed in the United States of America

QUM 10 9 8 7 6 5 4 3 2 1

Grateful acknowledgment is made to the editors
of the following publications in which these poems
first appeared or are forthcoming: *The Atlantic
Monthly:* "Passage," the final section of "To the
Animal in the Hole," and "Woodcock"; *Harvard
Review:* "Still Life with Pewter Pitcher"; *The
Larcom Review:* "Generatrix" and "When She
Lies Down at Night"; *Spirituality and Health:*
"Among Lilies" and "Mydas Fly."

Contents

I

Here 3

Among Lilies 4

Mole 6

Harvest Mouse 8

Tenderness 9

When She Lies Down at Night 10

The Chronicle of the Turkey 11

Passage 14

Mydas Fly 16

Woodcock 18

Quince 20

Generatrix 22

Low Tide 24

Possession 25

Mailbox 28

Collecting Hair 30

Turning Point 32

My Father's Lunch 35

II

To the Animal in the Hole 39

III

Still Life with Pewter Pitcher   49

Love Poem with Harbor View   51

Proof   54

Tundra   56

The Marvels of Insect Life   57

Café de Sol   61

The Seven Friendships   62

Cataract Canyon   66

First Apartment   74

Oasis   79

Casualty   83

Notes   88

I

Here

I lie in the last color left
from the other life —
bone white.
Everything emptied out of the room
because tomorrow the new light
with its new weight
will move in.

Wherever something had been left hanging
for too long, precise stains
remain: windows with no view,
or close-ups of bone,
which is not white
and not solid
but as full of openings

as the transformable space
between trees,
between trembling leaves,
when the body flings itself
from branch to branch.

Among Lilies

Indifferent to our arrival,
they go on culminating
in enviable pavilions

of delicate cream-white petals
streaked with warbler yellow
and yellow's flashy offspring

of fireworks. The air fills
with the twin scents of lemon
and vanilla from the time

before they were divided.
We offer a form of praise
resembling corridors of water:

We fountain. We cascade.
What fools we are, imagining beauty
might respond to its discovery.

In quieter corners of the garden,
other cultivars are satisfied to echo,
to underscore, to pursue

their own incremental pleasures
in an underlit world. Having sailed
into this Ilium of excess,

we haul out our stakes and wire,
our disciplinary powders,
bent on forestalling ruin.

But whose? Heedlessly, the lily gods
rain saffron pollen down
on our sweat-soaked shirts,

our backs bent and bending yet
in the breaking postures
of devotion.

Mole

This evening she's drilling
between raspberry canes,
mounds of mole-colored earth
crumbling behind her
like old ideas
of what a mole might be.

What is a mole? As a child,
I used to move earth
with my nose and with my hands
held close to my shoulders
like little paddles.
I practiced blindness, the better
to delve between pebbles.
Sick, in winter, I'd forage for air
inside an oxygen tent,
moling my way from one molecule
of breath to the next.

I observe the little accidents
of excavation — the barricade
erected by a rootball,
the way composted straw
collapses with a nudge.
Impossible not to think *monk*,
or *prisoner*, or *maiden*,
cloaked in homespun
to escape notice.

The mole goes after insects
with the anxious hunger
of a brushstroke.
If she's ever known
full-throated ease,
it would have been much farther down,
in the olooping chamber,
not up here, where only nerve
and a rough roof
keep her from my pitchfork.

Harvest Mouse

I hear it making light
of my deadly offerings
limned with fat.
A superior pause, and then
on to the hurricane candles
deep in their drawer.

My night above is so plain—
the usual human undoing
of the day—while downstairs
a body has made itself as thin
as a pencil to enter
by a flaw in the carpentry.

Ears, eyes, teeth, tail.
I can tell without looking
how the mouse knows my kitchen.
Skirts the burners,
dismisses the spices,
lolls in the fruit bowl:
a fur-bearing verb.

It will pulverize pearskin,
swallow raw almonds,
and leave shiny black pellets,
a trail of last-minute
satisfactions.

Tenderness

Last night the animals
beneath her window
crept out of hiding
to comb the dirt
from each other's fur.

Rising to watch,
she discovered the lilacs
lit from below by ivory vinca.
The street on the other side
of the trees continued
to contain its passing cars;
tenderly her teeth
let her tongue rest
against their curving backs.

Tonight when she lies
in bed again,
she will remember
the one kind thing
her grown daughter said today
after weeks of scrutiny,

and the moment at work
just now, when a stack
of Day-Glo folders
cascaded over her desk,
thrilling the white cubicle
with their descent.

When She Lies Down at Night

She tries to let the loneliness be another body.
What do you want of me? she asks,
as if to a troubled lover.
When there is no answer,
she lies beneath her own eyes
as if they were an uncertain ceiling,
wondering why she was given these ears,
this history, this imagination.
Sleep is the hardest work of the day.
The steadfast insomniac
tosses and turns on the empty side of the bed,
giving up nothing.

The Chronicle of the Turkey

Back now from his latest
wilderness, he lengthens his neck
    and lowers his head to extract
a pale meal from the grass in my yard.
    Before he swallows, he lifts
his chest toward the sun,
    Then he proceeds.

In another world, a robot
has been programmed to hunt
    for slugs: machine
with an appetite. My visitor
    is not at all mechanical;
when I startle him, he flourishes
    triumphant tailfeathers — chestnut,
topaz, and conjurer's black.
    The insects stop ticking.
The grass increases its green.
    The thoughts in my head
close up, an inferior fan.
    Which event in the future
will be explained by this tall bird
    the color of tea leaves?

He crosses the field
as he eats, each step intentional,
    as if momentum
required patience.

Knocking through the space
at the tip of his beak,
    cracking one sheer plane
to get through to the next,
    he advances, his everyday life
a repeat of the initial
    escape from the egg.

    Alice's question
to the Queen was "Can you keep
    from crying
by considering things?"
    What else is there to do?
The cutting-edge robot
    has been programmed
to consider slugs
    every time it gets
an electrical hunger
    in its gut.
To keep itself fed.
    To keep itself moving.

To keep myself
    from myself, I follow
the wild turkey.
    When he arrives
at the stone wall, he hoists

    himself up and over,
a statue transported
    by invisible genius.

As if there were cables attached.
    As if the turkey had been planning
all along to continue
    beyond the wall.
Had made the appropriate
    accommodations.
Is as aware as any hero
    of the monumental
gesture of farewell.
    How it will stay in the mind,
a flare of feathers,
    long after the bird
has vanished.

Passage

The hole sheared out of the roseleaf
by the leaf-cutting bee,

the jagged track above the grass
as the insect finds its rhythm,
dizzily trimming discs
from the leafy air,

the fencepost, still as a heron,
simultaneously considered
and rejected,

the crevice between shingles
also turned away from,

an abrupt descent to earth
below spear level,
below the congregations
of crickets,

to a chipped stone in the dirt,
its inviting lip,

the cavity precisely dark
and generous enough,

the tunneling and rolling,
the mixture of saliva and pollen,

the stowing and masticating,
the capping and cradling,
an arrangement by age

between meticulous forays
to carve yet another green seal
from the leaf of the rose,

the redundant rose,
its white weight
hauling every stem away
from a consenting trellis.

Mydas Fly

In mild sunlight, a concentration of velvet
and jet — even the face a midnight incident —

brings me to a halt: how nearly I missed
this simple-eyed fly, robotic on flowering mint,

as it probed for caterpillars and plump bugs
and took them in big black gulps.

I have been hunting for an act
this skillful, this unapologetic.

How does anyone get a job done well on a planet
chaotic with wind-riven scent?

Baroque ornament
in the service of elementary appetite:

even a gardener governed by distraction
recognizes her immediate sovereign.

The mydas fly. Slim this, ample that,
medallions of scarlet,

a tongue honed from splendid
guesswork to refined inquiry,

and, above all, a little humor:
antennae culminating in headphones

like exotic teardrops of tar. Who else will listen
to the drone of keeping oneself fed?

Woodcock

If you must possess something,
own it as she does her scrubby acre,
her seasonal work, the nomad's habit
of messing up the grass
until it looks like a careless footstep

and calling the fuss a nest
before laying two spotted eggs
upon which to fix
a native vigilance.

Claim it as she claims
these impatient evenings of early spring,
many footsteps in the weeds.
Try to acquire something
of her reckless voice,
the bright tines of the repeated bleeps
as she declares the precise coordinates
of all she wishes to conceal.

If necessary, take to the air
in ever more eccentric circles,
as her mate does, his nosedive
the last thing visible before dark.

And when you move on,
after the chicks have mastered

their own cryptic coloring,
migrate defiantly.
Be glad to be done
with this quarried-to-death terrain.

Quince

You should have seen the pale deer
advancing
through the banks of snow,
those angular knees
and the black nostrils
flaring.

Do you know
they keep their eyes open
as they wade
through the drifts?
The yellow iris
lights the way.

What wintering quince
could escape
their detection?
They remembered
my corner,
my luscious veneer
rosier than ever
in January moonlight.

They marched toward
a whirlpool of memory
in their tawny chests.
Late last summer, my twigs

had stirred their fur
as they arched over me
to reach ripe corn.

Their throats are tunnels.
Their teeth are tools.
They surround a branch
with breathless hunger
as they scrape through leafnode,
flowertip, and bark.

Before they go, they sever
the tender boughs.
They are still chewing
as they flick their tails
and take off.

Generatrix

A sparrow's indecisions —
or are they well-executed
excursions to invisible
   destinations? —
preoccupy the tree.

Nothing of the tree's
own doing. I should leave
the tree alone and not keep going back to it
with my sparrow-headed
   insistence.

Here. No, here.
Little flights in between
to nowhere.

If the beasts at Lascaux
were painted on the cave walls
to bring them in from the wild —
   a solicitation, at least,
if not a taming —

then why do I bring the flimsy sparrow
back to this porous page?
A common bird of dull plumage.
Hardly a bird at all,
   more a shift in the light,

only slightly less dark and more yielding
than the pine branch
where it works the day.

Spare row of what?
Arrangement of spares, of spheres,
in case of the inevitable
    shortage.

As mathematics is the only
infinite activity, this must be
something else.
    Now the sparrow's here,
at the fissure between trunk
    and branch,
now it's not,

    its come-and-go a kind of flickering
like that made by the oil light
that allowed the cave painters
and the hunters on the edge
    of the ellipse

    to use their attention
to bring some fiery-eyed motion
to a stop, or to proceed
    unsparingly
from a point the others
    had missed.

Low Tide

I walk the barrier beach
parallel to a ferry
quite far out at sea. We keep
the same speed, relatively;
at least we seem to advance
equally on this eastern
course, adamant as the knees
beneath a bronze colossus.
But when I reach the small rise
of a shellheap, I can see
the ferry flings out a fine
furrow, a compilation
of greens that leaves me jealous.
There is nothing I can do
to make the air demonstrate
how I have earned my passage.

Possession

A plain New England field,
no more topography
than a pine board, its lone

exuberance the cheer
of a male cardinal
among seed-heads. Again

today the field made room
for me, let me enter
by the spiraling path.

Do not mistake this one
arrival for the start
of anything. The field

lay in my head for years,
sprawling and oddly bound
as any memory.

I've made so many fields
of that first occasion
laid out between blue trees

that I can never leave
the field, not really, not
convincingly enough

to call any entry
the beginning. Today
I was caught trespassing

by the glossy boyfriend
of the equestrienne
who bought this field and more.

"You can't walk here," he said.
"We own it now." Own what,
I thought, as he dislodged

my morning's careless joy,
making way for a flood
of fantasized revenge:

I'd release starved deer ticks
and woodchucks in his field,
transplant poisonous vines . . .

Don't underestimate
the thrill of exceeding
one's own experience

of being an enemy.
It gave the field an edge.
No easy dominion

ever felt this certain,
this deep. When I go back
there next, I'll be a god.

Mailbox

Out here lives a man
who carries his box
as black as a mink
to its cedar post
every morning
and ties it in place
with cotton sashcord —
loop loop loop. If you
don't get out until
later in the day,
you can still see him,
only then he'll be
unwrapping the cord
and balling it up
like an Ace bandage.
He'll lift his mailbox
off its four-by-four
and tuck it under
his left arm without
checking for letters
and carry it in
to his mudroom, to
the kitchen table,
to an easy chair,
or all the way in
to his bed. I don't
know where he stops, but
somewhere in there he'll

snap open the door
like the rest of us
and run his hand back
and forward, back and
forward on the cool
black ridges of steel,
feeling for the edge
of luck, the lick of
comfort. He's got his
own names, I'm sure, for
what should be coming
to him any day.

Collecting Hair

One man's getting a shave;
somebody's son slumps
behind *Field & Stream*,
his pelt growing thicker
as he waits.
Only the unaltered hair
of men will do.
It keeps the deer away.

On the floor lie piles
of brown, gray, gold,
red filaments like lily stamens
and wiry blacks that build
to miniature volcanoes.
We are, after all,
earth-colored and reeking
of the earth beneath our feet.

I sweep up the undesired ends
that fell from the many strangers
sitting in these wide blue chairs
this afternoon, giving themselves
over to small talk
and their own sleek dreams
of success.

Those dreams, the way
they permeate every cell,

are what keep the deer
from my trees.
I smell the fertile urgency
as I sweep;

I'll smell it again
when I enclose the hair
in cheesecloth sacks
and string the bundles
from a few low branches,
like the eyes of ghosts
or like alarming testicles.

They are the same dreams
I enter when I touch
the blood-filled heads
of the men I love,
their wild hair rising
from body and from mind
and from the trackless wilderness
for which we have no name.

Turning Point

The very real buck
hauled his rack
up from a sea of apples.
I had done nothing more
than arrive in the field
a few seconds before my scent,
but how was the buck to know
if I was an armed god
or any little someone
on her way to market?

The huge animal, more huge
for having been caught by accident,
braced all four legs to hoist
his sprawling antlers up
like the ribs of a boat.
If I tell you
I saw fear cascading
from those prongs
in black waterfalls,
the still blacker silhouettes
of captives visible
in the torrent,
will you see it all as well?

The rest of the world
had already plunged

into the damp clover.
No, not everyone.
My father stood right there,
tall and ready for the first
day of deer season,
his young daughter
firm as a fencepost
at his elbow.

Speechless as ever,
he leaned toward me.
The world is full of lies,
but this is not one of them.
The buck was right there,
a straight shot,
and my father did not take it.
The gun barrel pointed to his feet,
a waste of readiness:

my one memory
of my father's passion
overcoming his skill.
Or have I imagined him
into this awkward morning
and invoked memory
to anchor the invention?

In the worst of all his nightmares,
Leonardo endured a steady stream
of tools dropping from the sky,
but he could rise to light a lamp
and sketch the shovels in free fall,
the accelerating calipers.

I wanted to step backwards,
to cede this moment
to the buck trembling
with territorial imperative,
but I had turned too slowly
and he raced ahead,
breaking free of my gaze
to clear the field.

The airy rack (had it weighed
nothing at all?) disappeared
into the shadowplay between saplings.
I bent down to fit my hand
over a few graspable apples.
And my father, long departed?
He will have forgotten the day,
if the dead forget.

My Father's Lunch

Saturday afternoon,
he'd sit at the kitchen table
in khakis and a workshirt.
White napkin, a beer, the serrated knife.
Pieces of prosciutto or headcheese
or kippered herring
layered on slabs of black bread.

Outside, the ripe hayfields
or the stacks of shutters
or the forest needing to be cleared
or the snow needing to be pushed aside
lay still as they waited for him
to finish his lunch.

For now he was ours,
whether he smelled of chokecherry,
tractor oil, or twine.
He'd washed his hands
with brown naphtha soap
and splashed water onto his face
and shaken it off like a dog.
He'd offer more ham, more bread
to anyone who sat down.

This was work, too,
but he did it slowly, with no impatience,
not yet reminding the older boys
that he'd need them later

or asking the smaller children
if we'd stored the apples
or shoved last year's hay
out of the wonderful window
to nowhere.

This was the interlude
of nearly translucent slices,
of leaning back in the smooth wooden chair
and wiping white foam from his lip
as the last beads of beer rose calmly
to the surface of the glass.
We could see it was an old meal
with the patina of dream
going back to the first days
of bread and meat and work.

All our lives, my brothers,
my sister, and I will eat
this same meal, savoring
its provisional peace,
like the peace in the grain room
after we'd scooped the grain
from the bins, and the sticky oats
and the agitated flakes of bran
had slipped back down into the soft valleys
where they would remain
until it was time to feed the animals again.

II

To the Animal in the Hole

1. BRIEF SIGHTING

You uncurl from underground,
more bent on blossoming
than any flower,

shake off ooil,
spy me,
swerve and flee,

leaving only this wide gap
with its ruffle of gravel,
its single inverted corolla.

2. ABOUT THE HOLE

A mineral enterprise,
small specimens gleaming
in the catchlight
of the hour,
hovering just where
they were tossed

until something like myself—
with my hunger, my impatience,
my lack of discipline—
stumbles upon the pickings,

or a heavier
or a differently flung rock
tilts them so a fresh
facet faces the light,

giving off the glint
of recent accomplishment,
the effort still being shaken off,
the new arrangement
astonishing only to me.

3. VISITATION

Trampled, leaf-stripped, bitten
to the ground,
each fruit inside the fence
broken or stolen,
whole rows of over-
anticipated greens
and high-strung succulence
demolished:

if the signs of your presence
were less damaging,
I would not be thrashing
through clipped leaves
and wilted vines

this morning, scouring
the aftermath
for your hillock heaped
with impudent stones.

4. LESSON IN HABITATION

In order to construct
your broad ramp,
you have been excavating
in one direction.
All the sand collects
in the northwest quadrant
of your entryway.
The remaining span goes undug.
This is how I know you are stubborn.

One source and one method:
a tenacious corruption
of solid into void,
void into home.

You and I come from a long line
of animals that use the world
in order to escape it.

5. THE NIGHT ABOVE THE HOLE

Advancing through the darkness
by comfortable guesswork—
path of sand more silver
than the grass,
air around the hemlocks
cooler than deciduous air—

I arrive at the space
I think of as yours:
emptiness
in the shape of a comet.

If you are diurnal,
as they say,
then surely you are here,
sweet, as you sleep,
accessory to nothing.

I wish I were wearing more white.
All the available moonlight
collects on the white cuffs
of my bathrobe,
the white tongues
of my running shoes.

When I have held still
for a long time,
some creature nearby resumes
its breathing and scratching,
gnawing at a source
larger and harder than itself.

I should not be here.
I see now you have a darker twin,
one I've missed in the daylight,
and she is trying to hollow out
a poor length of night
in which to dwell invisibly.

6. ORDINARY ENVY

When you are ready to enter
the everyday, you scramble
up over your gravelly spill,
tumbling into the sweet grass

where I hear you now,
tugging audibly at stalks
of shoulder-level clover.

I follow you
into your noon of pleasure
and imagine perching
on broad haunches.
When you bask on your boulder,
I bask on mine, trying to feel
too full to return home.

How ridiculous I must look
to you, practicing my rapture.
You prance back to the cool
reservoir of your hole

while I lie still and give up
my belief in this hour.
I am too skeptical,
too two-legged,
to disappear into the moment
as if it were mine.

7. TO THE ANIMAL IN THE HOLE

I've come back a few times,
seen you hurrying away
and, once, seen your eyes
the green of night.
Hope for this, hope for that—

who is free from such nonsense?
The small changes in the dirt
at your entrance,
the disappearance of grass:
I note these in your absence.

You should just stay where you are.
You and your dark house
will grow together.
You'll reach the walls,
they'll welcome your fur.
I'll know you're in there somewhere,
foraging invisibly.
Good for you, then.
Keep home.

III

Still Life with Pewter Pitcher

In the art of the everyday
one longs for distortion:
change in place of constancy.

So, when a girl's face appears
on the belly of the pitcher,
cheeks round with volume,

lips puckered in the diminutive
trumpet that can mean only No,
I take up the argument.

No what? No milk? No roses?
All right, then, emptiness
shall be yours. A minor rebellion.

Nothing's more receptive
than a pitcher, or more well
intentioned: all containment

and gracious delivery. Still,
the upstart trumpeter
is not content. Who summoned her?

Until now, I'd been grateful
the pitcher didn't leak; I chose it
because it poured beautifully. Is beauty

another thing I must unlearn?
The lip, the heft, the trembling water,
only figments of an old desire?

The girl's impatient pewter eye
directs me to the groaning streets
beyond this table and this window.

Who in the world is not waiting
to be touched and filled? Love something
your own size. Love the world.

Love Poem with Harbor View

There, splashed on the floor,
lies the light,
    helplessly yellow.
It has been out all night

    doing Lord knows
what, and now it is missing
    this morning's addition
to your new goatee,

    the exuberant darkness
forged from a good night's
    sleep. Outside, the ships
lashed to the wharves

    are slowly unloaded.
What do they know?
    Not even our names.
Cargoes accumulate on the quay,

    little self-absorbed cities
with eye-level skylines.
    I have woken before you.
You are too young to sleep beside,

    and yet you sleep
magnificently, the heat pouring

from your body's furnace.
In damp rooms

    all over Amsterdam,
restless eyes scour every visible
    surface for reassurance.
Perhaps my questions

    are not large enough,
if they can be satisfied
    by a single peninsula
of beard. One week ago,

    like a sweep's smudge,
the first shadow started
    below your tender lip.
Now, a field of black tulips

    prepares to unfold.
In a moment the buying and selling
    will begin. The light
will find its way

    to coffee pots and guilders
and hand-ground lenses,
    to the fruits of other lands
ripening beneath your window.

Poor impartial window.
Poor light, with its taste
   for glitter and glass.
Poor Holland not waking in your bed.

Proof

In 762, when the caliph al-Mansur
    asked for a city, his chief architect
(also geometer, astronomer, and mason)

scratched a generous circle in the desert
    west of the Tigris and placed the caliph
at its center, proceeding to outline

elegant avenues and cool gardens in naphtha,
    cottonseed, and ash. A pure picture
of the mind unbothered by human emotion.

Al-Mansur remained skeptical.
    Would this gameboard really become Abbasid's
brightest star? He looked blankly down

upon the pale saucers of oil that stood
    for reflecting pools, the piles of wool
fenced into caravansaries. Seeing nothing

but doodads and twigs, he ordered
    his servants to fetch mint tea and dates,
wondered out loud if history would remember him.

The architect had lived his whole life inside
    a few beautiful truths, like a nutmeat
nested beneath its glorious dome. He understood

the caliph's position hid the well-conceived city
   from him as day hides the stars. And so
he waited for the darkest hour of the night

before he set his beautiful idea on fire,
   the caliph seated at its center.
As the flames raced from conquest to conquest,

al-Mansur glowed with comprehension.
   "That's precisely what I mean by a city."
The next day the romance of Baghdad began.

Tundra

Because the jawbone once held canines
that stunned and halted duller flesh
and molars that flattened it for swallowing,

and formed the top half of the simple hinge
that is the body's instrument
of praise, alarm, and gratification;

but especially because the bone
had lain outside its original skull
long enough to be gnawed by numerous

predators and carried its assorted
toothmarks like a notched record
of impenetrable weather, all the while

cultivating a white so porous
it was almost blue, he pocketed the anonymous jaw,
not knowing whose hunger awaited him.

The Marvels of Insect Life

I

*". . . feed them until they spin cocoons or transform to a chrysalis,
then immediately kill and mount the freshly emerged specimen."*

She fed them
until they disappeared
into their windowless shacks,

and she kept on feeding them.
The work of the imagination
is to give itself away.

They could have been manufacturing
anything—excuses, counterfeit bills,
new versions of privacy.

She kept herself fresh for them.
She wanted to be ready to mount,
to examine. Oh yes, to capture.

When they grew too large
to keep indoors,
she slept at their side under stars.

She believed in them,
like white peaks hidden behind clouds,
or like the lithe bodies of the clouds themselves.

On some nights she could hear
the interior spinning,
a tentative extension of limbs.

In the end, they collapsed—
little dustquakes creating eddies of dust.
Her watching had weakened them.

She did what she could, resuming
her journey along the world's green stem,
aiming for the next desirable leaf.

2

*". . . a remarkable locust from the Congo, which was caught in the
act of catching and eating a mouse, and is now with its victim
preserved in the Natural History Museum at South Kensington."*

The great hunters conceal
their hunger. They wait until their prey
approaches them, looking for shelter,
or not looking at all.

The mouse was worn down
by a season of rain, perhaps,
or by the missionary's
persistent cleanliness.

The priest reclined on the terrace,
taking his tea black, regretting
whatever men regret in a colony
where everything has gone wrong.

Just then the insect struck.
It had been waiting among leaves
like a pool of rainwater,
when suddenly it shook out
its immense legs and seized
the soft neck.

The priest's benediction
still lingers over the captive pair,
the words "fatal chastisement"
inked onto a small white
water-stained flag.

3

*"In autumn, when frosty nights and increasing scarcity of insect food
teach the wasps that it will be impossible to rear their grubs into the
final stage, they are dragged from the cells in the combs, stung, and
carried into the fields, where they serve as food for birds."*

The wasps recognize their larvae
by the saliva that gathered

on the grubs' lower lips
and passed to the wasps
each time the grubs were fed.

They remember whose is whose
from the time when there was enough food
to go around.
Precisely adorned in black and gold,
the wasps work now like a guild of killers,
one larval C dangling
from each pair of claspers.

Ferrying their grubs over frosted grass,
they deposit them far in the distance,
where a few crows wait
nearly transparent with innocence.

Café de Sol

A pale starburst nearly invisible
in the northeast corner of his forehead —
she missed it, distracted by the babble
of arrival, until she leaned forward,
her spoon of preternaturally yellow
squash soup an offering. Yes, please, a sip
He hummed at the spice; she sought an elsewhere
and landed on his star. Just then she wished
the city light — so determined, so bright
as it leapt from sidewalk to windowsash —
would eclipse completely her raw delight,
leaving her free to ride his blaze at last.
Too late. The lesser darknesses that rule
ruled, and she trawled for starfruit in her soup.

The Seven Friendships

They were friends from the first look
the first day of work and friends
they would remain. Not lovers.
Never, though they thought of things
to whisper about all day.
At night, when they sat at home
hunting for something to say
to their actual lovers,
they longed to be back at work,
where the home life they described
to each other seemed larger,
funnier, more colorful.

They were playful as gods and,
at the same time, serious.
Once, in a car, on the way
to a conference, they worked out
the seven possible forms
of friendship between people
who aren't related by blood.

First: the fortunate friendship
of two who feel equally
attached but not attracted
to each other. No desire.
Instead, equilibrium,
a reliable membrane,
keeps them wholly separate
while holding them together.

You can always tell these two
in the kitchen: they can share
a cutting board — two different
sharp knives chopping two different
vegetables, and no one gets
in anyone else's way.

Second: the friendship founded
on suppressed desire. All
the accessorizing takes
the place of real nakedness.
The servant's invocations
to his master; the master's
adulation of the slave.
Michael Jackson / Liz Taylor —
yes — Regis and Kathie Lee.

Letter writers are the third,
their correspondence floating
safely above and beyond
their problematic bodies
like a vial of scented oil.
They use each other without
apology — an excuse
to shape the simplest moment
into something memorable
ending with "Write soon, write back,"
that frank plea for affection.

Then there is the electric
communion that's awakened
between two people vastly
different in age, like the
dowager one of them knew
who'd had to wait 'til she reached
ninety to meet a young child
she recognized as herself,
the adventuress she'd been.
At long last, the right playmate!

Fifth: the fireproof friendship
that has survived desire.
This includes all the ex-wives
and ex-husbands whose shared grief
unites them as love could not.
They drift back to each other,
grateful for a cup of tea,
for someone who remembers
that their first dentist in Troy
collected brass hose nozzles.

Next, a love of argument —
not bickering or nagging,
but the brainy brakes-without-
pads kind of arguing, no
attachment to conclusions,
no transparent right and wrong,
just the delirious pleasure

of competing for airspace
with someone you trust never
to take you personally.

And the seventh form? Friendship
based on the exchange of gifts,
preferably ridiculous.
Someone would get the idea
to buy odd salt and pepper
shakers, and once he'd purchased
the first set, a whole history
of silliness could begin.

That was when they stopped counting
and pulled off the interstate
on the way to the conference.
They found a small antique store,
Junkian Analysis—
really! —and in the windows
pairs of perfectly ugly
salt and pepper shakers shaped
like airplanes and bowling balls,
Roy Rogers and Dale Evans.
They liked the ceramic clams,
the Taj Mahal in Bakelite;
they loved the milkglass cabbage,
the jaguars, the shooting stars,
the stainless state of Vermont
side by side with New Hampshire.

Cataract Canyon

I'd always lived beside a listless river,
so when I left home at sixteen I turned
to Colorado: western rivers were wide,
I'd heard; you couldn't see the other side.
Fine. I wanted to be out there, going
where tremendous rivers went. The sixties.
Everyone I met was a practicing
teenager in jeans and a peasant smock.
In Carbondale, the people I stayed with
made everything from scratch — vests and earrings,
mugs, looms, sourdough starter, their own yurt.
At night my new friends and I strained jellies
or swallowed little buttons of peyote,
threw up, and lay down in the fragrant sage
to wait for visions.

                  I can't remember
who made the first mold, but soon we were all
layering resin over fiberglass,
running from the shed to avoid the fumes
and scratching at the threads of angelhair
that bit into our wrists like prickly heat.
After a few weeks we had nine kayaks.
We sewed spraycovers from waterproof cloth
and bought wetbags at the army-navy.
Two wetbags each: in one we packed small sacks
of whole wheat flour to make chapatis,
some dried apricots, and nuts; in the other
a change of clothing and a wool blanket.

We'd give ourselves two weeks to shoot the canyon—
forty miles, but in early summer still
a lot of snowmelt in the river, or so
we'd heard.

       People were always stopping by
who'd just run the Gunnison or the Snake;
all the talk was about water levels,
a good spot to leave the truck, where to climb
to rappel our boats into the canyon.
We'd boil the brown riverwater to drink
and forage for edible greens and roots.
This didn't seem preposterous at the time.
The toughest-looking men had turned foolish
at the mention of a pink sandstone gorge
or a side canyon where they'd hiked back up
until they'd found a thundering cascade
or sighted bighorn sheep.

             I never knew
how much was true, but the pure rhapsody
softening their faces was true enough.
And the fact that I was going to wear
a blue floral-print two-piece bathing suit
through the western plateau's roughest water
never struck me as impractical.
The other girl wore a string bikini.
She'd kayaked before, and in the duckpond
she helped me practice my Eskimo roll,

teaching me a way to use the paddle
to compensate for my awkward body.

The man who'd showed us how to build our boats
told us helmets would make us too complacent.
We were supposed to roll ourselves back up
before we blacked out or struck a boulder.
He took us to milder rivers—the Green,
the Yampa—and we practiced rescuing
ourselves from the unknown that lay in wait
beneath the opaque surface. Once we got
confident, he took us to worse water,
and worse. He wanted us to learn to read
the water. To read it right.

                              I'd never
studied water for its story. The river
I grew up beside was slow—no, sluggish:
one looked at it and thought of other things
or tried to escape the restless current
of one's own thoughts. It dabbled at its bank.
But not these big western rivers: they drilled
themselves into one's mind as into stone,
leaving the same vertical walls, the same
cliffs and buttes and narrowing passageways
where the water of half a continent
compressed into a deep delirium.

I'd stand on the rocks, skittish as a hare,
unable to hear the others through the roar,
and try to read where this wild force of will
wanted to consume me, and where it would
relent and shoot me forward like a speck
of bark. Each boulder, each invisible
shift in depth or volume, threw the water
into a distinctive chute or sinkhole
or whirlpool. Ruined tree trunks could create
a wall of water the color of cement;
some enormous waves moved so crazily
they threw out metallic whitecaps or caused
eddies to form that beat their way upstream.

Once we watched a dead cow in a whirlpool:
the helpless carcass flew out of the froth
like a nickel, heads or tails, and was pitched
back down into the swirl to start again.
The only way to escape a whirlpool,
we learned, was to leave your boat and dive down
into the riverbed, swimming like hell
downstream.

I knew I'd never do that.
We were supposed to make one solid plan
and stick to it. We had to carve a map
in our minds of where we'd go and how — stroke,
angle, timing — and then we had to enter

our boats and ride that made-up map over
real water with a purpose of its own.
If I'd possessed a speck of confidence
before that summer, it was as a smart-
ass: I was clever at undermining
the authority of a dull adult
or numbing a hesitant opponent.
Now the nearly uncontainable roar
of the Colorado as it shot down
through the black walls of Cataract Canyon
was enough to collapse the scaffolding
I'd come to identify as courage.
I was terrified, and the roaring river
could have cared less if I plunged into it
or not. Most days I didn't.

                  I believe
I'm one of the few people to have walked
the length of Cataract Canyon carrying
a kayak on her shoulders. I portaged
almost every rapid — the ones with only
a narrow ledge to crawl across, the ones
strewn with angular boulders or talus
so slippery it tricked my feet like seaweed.
I'd stand up high with the others to read
the river; while they pointed out their runs,
I'd envision a private disaster —
suffocation, flood, or lethal impact —

as I rode toward the inevitable
in the thin-sided boat whose sunflower
yellow I'd applied with a carefree stroke.

After I'd watched my new friends paddle through,
I'd start the long, hot walk to the quiet
water below. They were always down there,
triumphant in their brightly colored boats,
flashing peace signs and hugging each other,
pushing the hair back from their brave faces.
"Next time, you're coming with us," they'd holler,
and I'd yell, "Sure!"

                    not meaning it at all.
There was a boy among us, audacious
as the river. Arthur. He'd left high school
and burned his draft card in San Francisco.
Now he worked in a molybdenum mine
up in Climax. I admired his skill;
he offered me advice I dared to take,
and I improved slowly; but I was sure
he thought I was a coward. He was strong,
all muscle, and he walked like a dancer,
using gravity to lift himself
into the air. On the water, his boat
belonged to his slender hips: one shimmy
sent him flying through the obliging waves.

I was the only one who knew he used.
He'd let me know about the heroin
because I was weak and scared, I believed,
because I had a habit of my own —
fear — that had brought me no comfort at all.
He was the first person to let me see
the limitations of confidence, to let
me see that fear and hesitation might
just lead me closer to another person,
to another part of nature,

                    the fresh,
sweet smell of a strong young man
giving up beside the silty river.
Giving up what, exactly, I could not say.
I wanted the drug he lived by — its heat —
but I wanted it from his lizard's tongue,
and when we sat together by the fire,
as the others slept, he never touched me;
he hardly spoke. Sometimes his agate-striped
eyes took up the firelight and cast it
back into the darkness; as he unpacked
his gear, he'd recollect one precious thing
that I'd done well that day. Then, the wetbag
open in his lap, he'd lay his strange goods
on a crimson bandanna and begin.

After he'd shot up and released the strap,
Arthur sat back and let himself be flooded
with a torrent of passivity
I'd never seen in any animal.
A sheen came over him as he lay there,
a white ruin, like a whole piñon trapped
in the river, season after season,
worn down to its skeletal origins.
I'd never seen the stuff that got an addict
through a day. I wanted to glow a bit
from his compliment. Or convince myself
that he was safe like this.

                             Impossible.
Instead, I crept around his ravaged form
and cleaned up the sad paraphernalia
so no one would find it in the morning.
Every morning, he woke up with the fight
back in his eyes, one danger as seductive
as the next, while I lifted the yellow boat
onto my shoulder and crossed a rockslide
or a mile of prickly pear, anything
to avoid the wild and senseless river.

First Apartment

A door slams, a child cries, and its father
shouts, "Shut up, cunt, or I'll mash your balls in."
Moving day, Charlestown, 1975.
The world was divided into townies
and everyone else: white, black / us, the law.
But in our building there were gentler laws.
Downstairs lived a quiet bookie who kept
his sister and his mother in grand style;
one floor above, a woman left each night
to box candy at the Schrafft's factory,
returning in time to cook hot cereal
for her husband, a vet, who hadn't yet
recovered from service in Korea.
Afternoons, he liked to serenade her
as she slept. Their son was a Marine;
I knew because his mother asked me once
if I thought oatmeal cookies would survive
the trip to Quantico and not get stale.

I was learning to marry my young self
to an idea called wife and to a man
and to the black and white of love before
I grew brave enough to see its subtler shades.
Because I had no answers, no solid
word for any day, plain or exotic,
that flew by, I soaked up all the language
of the stairwell, the street, the *Boston Globe*.
At work I asked people how long they sat

at the table after dinner. Did they
ever wish they'd left the radio on?

I spied on everyone, trying to fathom
the mysteries of marriage: How could
I go on reading while he spackled walls?
Was it all right to leave without saying
where I was going, without having somewhere
to go? When would I recognize myself
again? When would I know which conventions
were worth imitating, at least until
we devised an original union
of our own? And what was one marriage worth
when the streets were streaked with anti-busing
slogans and stones flew against the windows
where black children clutched their satchels and wept?

A few things happened that we won't forget,
most of them violent. One night, woken
by a gunshot, we watched from our ivy-
covered bedroom window as the owner
of the corner package store, his arm poised
on the roof of our car, fired steadily
at someone huddled on the stoop next door.

Early that spring, I planted a single hill
of canteloupe on our fire escape
in defiance of all natural logic

and because the one thing I'd always done
was grow things. From their makeshift trellis
the vines wandered through the kitchen window
to the slightly buckled imitation-
brick linoleum and from there into
the parlor, where my husband had brought down
a ton of coal dust by trying to clear
the chimney, a fire in the fireplace
being his idea of a working marriage.

Then came the summer morning when two cops
were knocking at our door. "Excuse us, ma'am.
Are you Mrs. . . . ?" Across the arm of one
I saw my husband's suitcoat soaked with blood.
"Struck by a car," they said. "Nothing serious,
but the head's a bleeder, does it ever
bleed." "Which hospital?" I yelled. "Just tell me
where you took him." Mass. General, they said,
without bothering to budge. Instead,
the heavier one handed me the coat
and told me I better get it soaking
in cold water quickly, before it stained.

Like a wife, I thought, offering advice,
but as I raced across the bridge to Boston
I was a wife in love. I didn't want
my husband hurt. I didn't want him touched
by cars. I wept at the idea of chrome

piercing the head I'd held an hour ago,
when a spell of drenched pleasure had obscured
the blare of others hurrying to work.
I knew then why I'd married him, why we'd
have children we'd protect from everything
but love, but us.

                I heard his laughter first,
before I saw him, and for a second
I hated the fact that he was laughing
when I'd been wild with fear. But that huge laugh
from inside the waiting room had kept me
up nights doubled over in breathless glee,
had pulled me back from the nameless places
I go to when left too much alone.
There he was, sitting up, animated,
his arm around a very small woman
in chaps, their heads identically bandaged.
She could have been the therapeutic doll
that comes with every injury to the head.

In the same instant I saw that he was fine,
I realized he was doing the one thing
we did best for each other—collecting
a good story. He began to tell me
in the cab on the way home, and he finished
in the vaguely dusty afternoon light
of our railroad apartment, in my arms.

She turned out to be the only female
jockey at Suffolk Downs; she'd been riding
a skittish colt; early morning was when
she liked to work him, but he had thrown her
so often the other jockeys called him
"Slingshot." Which made her "Pebbles," a direct
reference to *The Flintstones* and an insult.
This was her third emergency this month;
she'd shown my husband the other purple scars.
Still, she'd take a horse over a man
any day, she swore. A horse was trainable.
As he told me this and as I listened,
the canteloupe ripening to inscribed
moons above the fire escape, my husband
and I lay together in the first plumb
moment of our long initiation
into love, a moment and a union
that would outlast the tenuous marriage.

Oasis

Sparrow and starling and cowbird.
The ordinary ones drop down
    from a white sky
to the promise of water
    in a shallow bowl.
Lined up on its rim, they hover
    like the great-aunts and -uncles
I've watched in a dog-eared photo:
    Atlantic City, early in the century,
the whole gang striking sideshow poses
    in swimsuits of long-sleeved wool,
"Jeffries Baths" block-printed
    on their broad white belts,
an improbable donkey in their midst.

    Splashing and spattering,
mouths hollow with thirst,
    with pleasure. In the photograph
and in the birdbath, modesty
    takes a vacation.
They were a family of coal miners,
    their sisters and cousins,
and those were the glory days
    before they knew how much
would elude them.
    No one had been killed in a blast
yet, or seen her baby swallow lye,

or driven himself, drunk,
into a tamarack.
    None of the black dust was visible.

    In that one stolen moment,
they sparkled, brazen as finches,
    young and nearly aristocratic
as they flexed their wiry muscles
    below the boardwalk.
The chaperone aunt, screened
    in white muslin, napped
beneath her striped awning.
    Later, someone swirled their names
at their feet in sepia ink —
    Gerald and Ira and James.
Maeve, Bessie, and Lil.

    You can almost hear the barrage
of minor insults that preceded
    the photograph,
washing them clean of reserve.
    A whole week of foolishness
at the bathhouse with its tasseled donkey:
    what that must have meant
to those pale men and women
    brought up to ply one dark seam
all their lives.

From the terracotta shore
of the birdbath, one of the large birds
    bumps a smaller one into the bowl
and two robins already bathing
    slap sheets of water over them all.
I could almost hear the superior aunt
    rising and crying out in high holiday
humor, "If you're so grand,
    then what are you doing
sharing your bath?"

    This evening the world will not
improve much, but with luck
    these birds will relieve the itch
where feathers break from flesh.
    They'll return to their branches
to deliver one last song before sleep.
    Their vacation over,
Joe and Carrie and Hazel must have taken
    the train back to Pittsburgh,
their hair streaked with salt,
    the white sand heating up
between their toes. Leaning their heads
    on each other's shoulders,
they never spoke about tomorrow;
    they kept on simmering
in their time-wasting dizziness,

as if they had nothing better to do
than float in the ocean and blow
     clear green bubbles
before disappearing under the waves.

Casualty

For the few hours
while they are still trying
    to save him,
strangers will be begging for a name,
    but for now he is alone,
slumped over the steering wheel
    here in the emergency lane
where he has managed to guide
    the car before blacking out.
He doesn't think he hit anyone.
    The last thing he saw in the windshield
was his mother fifty years ago
    tossing him a baseball.
Her arm slender and beautiful,
    pitching the ball with its pink seams,
his whole body bent to receive
    the whirling weight.

He comes from a long line of people
who tried to get one thing right.
    They'd open a little grocery store
or pass a correspondence course
    and try not to appear too ambitious
or too hopeful. They'd work
    every minute, appreciating the chances
of failure, and still they'd fail.
    Stranded here, not yet dead,
custodian of collapsed hopes,

he recalls all his relations
who never saved a nickel
    but could imagine success
as if it were a bluebird in their hands.

    I hear him. Can you hear him
whispering to himself as he waits
    in the driver's seat for something to end?
A regular weekday in Seattle.
    The accident will not bear reporting.
No shrines will go up in the weeds
    where the soft tires slurred to a halt.
His sister, the one who phones me
    with the news, didn't even realize
her brother had come to Seattle; if it hadn't been
    for the driver's license,
discovered hours later in the trunk,
    she'd never have known.

    All our lives the earth wants us back,
I can hear him telling the steering wheel,
    his forehead pressed against
the black leatherette stitches. It lets us rise
    knee-high, waist-high,
even shoulder-high, and then
    it pulls us back down to its side.
In the darkness, he's troubled
    by the scent of pine

dangling from the rearview mirror;
    his tool belt turns over
like a dog in its dreams.
    The only thing stopping him
is fatigue. How can a person
    be too tired to die?

    In a few minutes, someone
will find him. Later, someone else
    will phone his sister.
The doctors will huddle around her
    with their bolt-of-lightning
analogy: it burned through his brain
    like a tree. The police will come.
Thank God he didn't kill anyone
    on his way out. Do you know
his license had expired? No insurance.
    No registration. She knew nothing.
She hadn't heard from him in years.
    None of the names we give
to these people—drifters, loners,
    the homeless—will ever apply
to the older brother who'd been living
    right there, in her city,
without calling her.

    A few days after she buried him,
she found the address of a lumberyard.

They'd hired her brother
to assemble wooden pallets.
    This information led
to the last man to see him alive.
    "We let him sleep in the yard,"
he told the inquiring sister,
    pointing to the quonset hut
next to the guard dogs' house.
    "He was good with the dogs,
good with engines, always minded
    his own business.
He disappeared now and then,
    but who doesn't?"

    In the car beside the highway,
he is still trying, unsuccessfully,
    to disappear. He's not sure
whether to back off
    or to plunge forward. He's afraid
he's forgotten something,
    one of those small essentials —
the keys, the list — that you grab
    just as you're leaving.
His mother had a good pitching arm
    but terrible aim. The one time
she hit him with a hardball,
    it felt like this, his eyes

driven so far back into his head
    that he couldn't see her
running toward him, but he knew
    she was coming to help;
he could just make out his name—
    the Jim, the Jimmy—
skimming the darkness
    between them.

Notes

"Mole": "full-throated ease" is from Keats's "Ode to a Nightingale."

"The Marvels of Insect Life": the three quotations are from *The Marvels of Insect Life*, edited by Edward Step (New York: McBride, Nast & Company, 1915).

© Debi Milligan

Erica Funkhouser is the author of four collections of poetry, including *Sure Shot and Other Poems* and *Natural Affinities*. She has received three awards from the Poetry Society of America, and her poems have been published in magazines and literary journals, including *The Atlantic Monthly, The New Yorker,* the *Paris Review, Ploughshares,* and *Poetry.* She teaches at the Massachusetts Institute of Technology.